W9-CEL-942

THE
LIGHT BULB

Chris Oxlade

Chicago, Illinois

www.heinemannraintree.com
Visit our website to find out more information about Heinemann-Raintree books.

To order:
☎ Phone 888-454-2279
💻 Visit www.heinemannraintree.com to browse our catalog and order online.

Edited by Louise Galpine and Laura Knowles
Designed by Philippa Jenkins
Illustrations by Oxford Designers & Illustrators
Original illustrations © Capstone Global Library
   Limited 2012
Picture research by Mica Brancic
Originated by Capstone Global Library Limited
Printed and bound in China by CTPS

15 14 13 12 11
10 9 8 7 6 5 4 3 2 1

Library of Congress Cataloging-in-Publication Data
Oxlade, Chris.
   The light bulb / Chris Oxlade.
      p. cm.—(Tales of invention)
   Includes bibliographical references and index.
   ISBN 978-1-4329-4880-1 (hc)—ISBN 978-1-4329-4889-4 (pb)   1. Light bulbs—Juvenile literature. I. Title.
   TK4351.095 2012
   621.32'6—dc22   2010036498

Acknowledgments
We would like to thank the following for permission to reproduce photographs: Alamy pp. **9** (© Georgios Kollidas), **17** (© Interfoto), **20** (© The Print Collector), **26** (© Richard Levine), **27** (© Modern Design); Corbis p. **4** (© NASA); Getty Images pp. **5** (Photodisc/David Toase), **6** (Science & Society Picture Library), **7** (Hulton Archive), **8** (Science & Society Picture Library), **12** (Mike Kemp), **14** (Archive Photos/Welgos), **16** (Archive Photos/George Eastman House), **18** (Hulton Archive/ Fox Photos), **19** (Hulton Archive), **22** (Hulton Archive/ General Photographic Agency), **25** (Science & Society Picture Library); Science Museum p. **11** (Science & Society Picture Library); Science Photo Library p. **13** (Adam Hart-Davis), Shutterstock pp. **21** (© Diego Cervo), **23** (© Elnur); Smithsonian Institution p. **15** (Archives Center, National Museum of American History).

Cover photograph of the world's largest incandescent lamp (c. 1935) reproduced with permission of Getty Images/Hulton Archive.

We would like to thank Peter Smithurst for his invaluable help in the preparation of this book.

Every effort has been made to contact copyright holders of material reproduced in this book. Any omissions will be rectified in subsequent printings if notice is given to the publisher.

Disclaimer
All the Internet addresses (URLs) given in this book were valid at the time of going to press. However, due to the dynamic nature of the Internet, some addresses may have changed, or sites may have changed or ceased to exist since publication. While the author and publisher regret any inconvenience this may cause readers, no responsibility for any such changes can be accepted by either the author or the publisher.

CONTENTS

Look for these boxes

Any words appearing in the text in bold, **like this**, are explained in the glossary.

Biographies

These boxes tell you about the life of inventors, the dates when they lived, and their important discoveries.

Setbacks

Here we tell you about the experiments that didn't work, the failures, and the accidents.

EUREKA!

These boxes tell you about important events and discoveries, and what inspired them.

TIMELINE

2011—The timeline shows you when important discoveries and inventions were made.

LIGHT IN OUR LIVES

We have light bulbs in our homes and schools, and in offices and factories. Outside, we light up yards, sidewalks, roads, and tunnels with light bulbs. Lights such as traffic signals give us information. The light bulb is one of the most important inventions of all time.

The light from street lamps in busy towns and cities can be seen from space.

Before electric light

Humans lived for many thousands of years without electric light. Before the discovery of fire, the only source of light at night was the Moon and stars. The oil lamp was invented about 70,000 years ago. It was a shallow stone dish filled with animal fat. Moss was used as a **wick**, where the flame burned. The candle, which burns wax, was invented about 5,000 years ago, probably in Egypt.

4

around 70,000 years ago—
The first animal fat lamps are used

By the 1800s, oil lamps looked very different from the early stone dishes used for lighting.

EUREKA!

Nobody knows exactly when humans discovered fire, but it was probably more than one million years ago. Early humans took fire from natural fires caused by lightning. Firelight allowed them to live in caves, where they were safer than being outside. By about 9,000 years ago, humans had invented ways of making fire. One way was to rub sticks together. The **friction** between the sticks made them hot enough to smolder.

Gas lamps

Gas was first used for lighting in ancient China, by about the 100s CE. Then, in the 1790s, gas lamps were also invented in England. These gas lamps burned gas made by heating coal. Gas was supplied along pipes. At first, gas lamps were used to light streets in larger cities and towns. Then, they were gradually installed in buildings. They had to be lit each evening. In homes they sometimes caused explosions.

around 9,000 YEARS AGO— Humans invent fire-making tools

around 5,000 YEARS AGO— The candle is invented in Egypt

around 2,000 YEARS AGO—Gas is used for lighting in China

30,000 YEARS AGO

10,000 YEARS AGO

Light bulbs need electricity to work. This means they were not possible until inventors had discovered a source of electricity to use. For hundreds of years, people knew how to make electricity, but only enough to make small sparks. Then in 1800, Italian scientist Alessandro Volta made the first **battery**. It was made up of copper and zinc discs, each separated by paper soaked in acid. This arrangement is now known as a voltaic pile.

This is a copy of one of Alessandro Volta's batteries.

EUREKA!

Luigi Galvani was a friend of Alessandro Volta. He carried out experiments with what he called "animal electricity." He made a frog's leg twitch by touching the frog's nerve with a copper hook attached to an iron stand. Volta realized that the two metals (copper and iron) were making electricity. This gave him the idea for his battery.

6

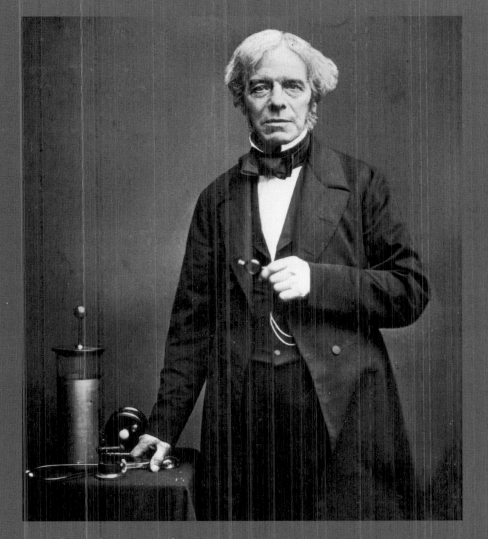

Michael Faraday (*1791–1867*)

Michael Faraday was an English scientist who invented the **electric motor** in 1821. A few years later he discovered that moving a magnet through a coil of wire made electricity flow through the wire. In 1831 Faraday used this knowledge to invent a **dynamo**, which generated electricity when he turned its handle. Other inventors took Faraday's idea and improved it. By the 1870s, they had designed **generators** that could produce large amounts of electricity.

1801—Humphry Davy demonstrates an incandescent lamp (see page 12)

1807—Humphry Davy invents the first electric **arc lamp** (see page 8)

1810

THE ARC LAMP

The **arc lamp** was the first sort of electric light. The arc lamp's bright light came from a spark of electricity that jumped through the air between two sticks of carbon, called **electrodes**.

The arc lamp was invented by Humphry Davy in 1807, but it wasn't used for many decades. From 1878 arc lamps lit the streets of Paris. They had to be checked regularly and needed lots of electricity. Houses did not have the electricity supply needed for arc lamps. Even if they had electricity, the lamps would have been too bright to be used in the home.

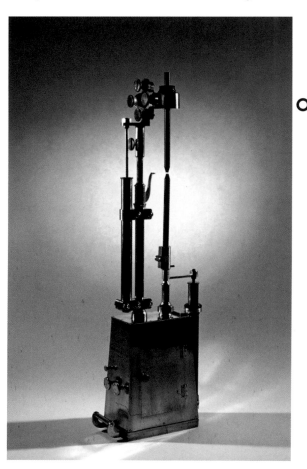

This arc lamp made light in an English lighthouse in the 1860s.

Setbacks

The arc lamp needed a powerful supply of electricity to make it work. In 1807 Humphry Davy used 2,000 **batteries** joined together to make just one arc lamp light up. Using this many batteries was impractical. It was another 50 years before electricity **generators** powerful enough to work arc lamps were developed.

1815—Humphry Davy invents the miner's safety lamp

1816—Thomas Drummond invents limelight (see page 13)

Humphry Davy *(1778–1829)*

Humphry Davy was born in Penzance, England. He was the son of a woodcutter. He investigated heat, light, and electricity, and he soon became well known for his new theories. The arc lamp was not the only lamp he invented. After investigating the causes of explosions in mines, Davy designed a miner's safety lamp that saved many lives. Davy also made an early light bulb (see page 12). He was the leading British scientist of his day.

1821—Michael Faraday invents the **electric motor** (see page 7)

THE INCANDESCENT BULB

For more than 100 years, the **incandescent light bulb** was the most common source of light. It is still in use today, although it is being replaced by modern **energy-efficient** light bulbs.

The word **"incandescence"** means a bright light given out by a substance when it is very hot. Inside an incandescent light bulb is a thin strand of material called a **filament**. When electricity flows through the filament, the filament gets so hot that it glows brightly.

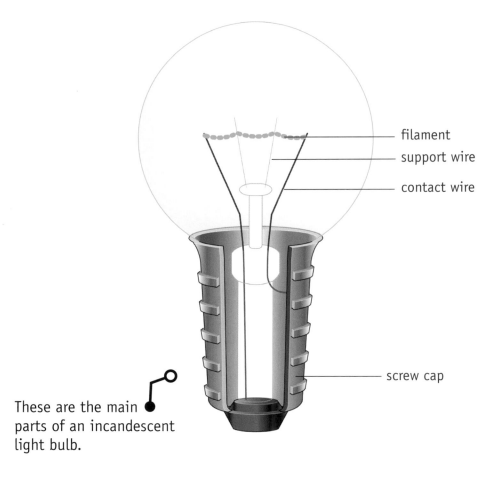

filament

support wire

contact wire

screw cap

These are the main parts of an incandescent light bulb.

1830s—Michael Faraday discovers how to make a **dynamo** to produce electricity (see page 7)

1840s—Joseph Swan makes experimental light bulbs (see page 19)

1830

1840

Hermann Sprengel's vacuum pump was a groundbreaking step in the development of light bulbs.

EUREKA!

The problem of making a vacuum inside a light bulb was finally overcome in the 1870s, when German Hermann Sprengel invented the **mercury** vacuum pump (now called the Sprengel pump). It used mercury dripping through tubes to suck air out of a bulb.

Bulb problems

Scientists knew about incandescence in the early 1800s. But it took nearly another 80 years before a successful light bulb was made. Why did it take so long? There were two problems. First, inventors needed to find a material to use for a filament that would glow brightly but not melt. Second, they had to stop the filament from burning up in the air. That meant putting the filament in a glass bulb and sucking the air out of the bulb to make a **vacuum**. At the time, there wasn't a good enough pump to do this.

1845—John W. Starr takes out a **patent** for a light bulb (see page 13)

1850

Early experiments

In 1801 Humphry Davy, inventor of the **arc lamp**, also demonstrated the first incandescent light. Davy used **platinum** strips for his filament, which quickly burned up in the air. Over the next few decades, inventors used various materials for filaments. Some put their filaments inside glass tubes with as much air as possible sucked out. But none of these experimental light bulbs lasted very long.

In Canada in 1874, Henry Woodward and Mathew Evans invented a light bulb with carbon filaments. They took out a **patent** for it in Canada and the United States. Having a patent on an invention means that it is against the law for anybody else to copy the idea. The bulb worked well, but they did not manage to sell many.

You can see the glowing filament in this modern light bulb.

1855—Heinrich Geissler demonstrates the principle of gas discharge (see page 23)

1860s—The first electricity **generators** are built (see page 7)

1850

1860

Limelight

One successful form of incandescent lighting in the 1800s was known as limelight. It was invented in 1839 by Scottish engineer Thomas Drummond. Limelight was made by heating a block of **lime** until it glowed brightly. Because it could be directed as a beam of light, it was often used as a spotlight in theaters.

Setbacks

U.S. inventor John W. Starr designed two light bulbs. One had a platinum filament in a glass bulb. The other had a carbon filament in a vacuum and was patented in 1845. Unfortunately, these lamps were not practical for everyday use. Starr was working on new bulbs when he died from **tuberculosis** in 1846.

This is an early limelight lamp. Burning oxygen and hydrogen gas made the block of lime glow brightly, but it was also dangerously explosive.

1870s—Hermann Sprengel invents his vacuum pump (see page 11)

EDISON'S LIGHT BULB

In the 1880s, a U.S. inventor named Thomas Alva Edison turned the **incandescent light bulb** from an experimental idea into a money-making success. Edison is often said to be the inventor of the light bulb. In fact he wasn't, but he did take other inventors' ideas and improve them.

In 1878 Edison designed a light bulb that had a **platinum filament**. However, the design was complicated, and the light bulb switched itself off if it overheated. So Edison experimented, using various **carbonized** plant fibers as filaments. Carbonizing removed some of the substances from the fiber, leaving mostly carbon behind. Edison had successes with carbonized paper and carbonized cotton.

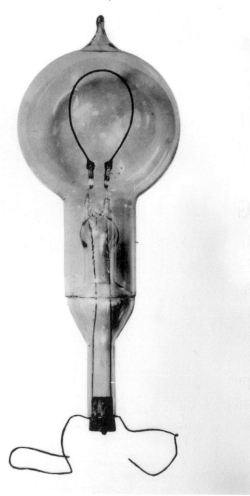

This is an early Edison light bulb. It was not plug-in or screw-in, but rather mounted on a wooden base and designed to be put on a table, like a table lamp.

1874—Henry Woodward and Mathew Evans take out a **patent** for a light bulb (see page 12)

1876—Thomas Edison opens a research laboratory (see page 16)

1878—Edison makes a light bulb with a platinum filament

1879—Joseph Swan demonstrates his first working light bulb (see page 18)

1870

1880

The first place Edison's light bulbs were installed was on a steamship, the SS *Columbia*.

Glow lamps

In 1880 Edison formed the Edison Electric Lamp Company to make bulbs, which he called "Glow Lamps." Edison soon changed to using carbonized bamboo fibers for his filaments. He used a Sprengel pump (see page 11) to pump the air out of his bulbs.

EUREKA!

Edison worked hard to find the best material for the filaments in his light bulbs. He collected samples of thousands of different plant fibers, carbonized them, and tested them in bulbs. Eventually he chose carbonized bamboo for his bulbs.

1880—Edison forms the Edison Electric Lamp Company

1882—Edison opens an electricity generating station (see page 17). Joseph Swan starts the Swan Electric Light Company Ltd (see page 18).

1883—Thomas Edison and Joseph Swan form the Edison and Swan United Electric Light Company (see page 20)

1890

Thomas Alva Edison (1847–1931)

Thomas Alva Edison was born in Milan, Ohio. His first job was as a newspaper seller on the railroads. He set up a chemistry laboratory in a train's caboose, but was thrown out when he set the caboose on fire. In 1876 Edison set up a laboratory at Menlo Park, New Jersey. He employed inventors, engineers, and scientists to help him. In addition to the light bulb, Edison invented the phonograph (the first sound-recording machine), a telephone transmitter, a fire alarm, and the kinetoscope (for viewing moving pictures). When he died, Edison held more than 1,000 **patents**.

1898—Daniel McFarlan Moore makes the first successful gas discharge lamp (see page 23)

Power for bulbs

In the 1880s, nobody had an electricity supply at home. Edison realized that he wasn't going to sell any light bulbs if people had no source of electricity to make them work. So he set up a power station in New York. It was called the Pearl Street Station. When it opened in 1882, it was the world's first commercial power station. Its **generator** produced enough electricity for 800 bulbs in houses, offices, and factories. Edison also sold the cables, **meters, fuses**, and sockets that people needed to connect to the electricity supply.

This is a model of Edison's Pearl Street power station.

1902—Georges Claude invents a way of getting neon and argon gases from the air (see page 23)

1907—Captain Henry Joseph Round discovers that diodes can give out light (see page 25)

1909—The General Electric Company starts making bulbs with **tungsten** filaments (see page 21)

1910

LIGHT BULB RIVALS

Thomas Edison was not the only inventor to successfully make and sell light bulbs. In the 1860s, British inventor Joseph Swan had also started making light bulbs.

Swan tried many different materials for **filaments** before settling on cotton thread treated with acid. The filaments were only one-tenth of a millimeter thick. Like Edison, Swan used a Sprengel pump (see page 11) to create the **vacuum** in his bulbs. He also found a way to make filaments last longer—by heating the filament as the air was pumped out of the bulb.

Swan **patented** his light bulb and demonstrated it in public in 1879. In 1882 he set up the Swan Electric Light Company Ltd to make bulbs to sell. Swan not only made bulbs, but also installed electric lighting in buildings.

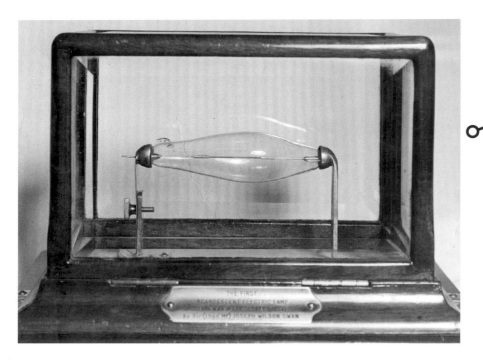

This is Joseph Swan's first **incandescent light bulb**.

1910—George Claude makes the first neon lamp (see page 23)

Joseph Swan *(1828–1914)*

Joseph Swan was born in Sunderland, England. His first job was as a pharmacist, and he became an expert on chemicals for photography. Swan started experimenting with light bulbs in the 1840s, thinking they would be useful for photography. He tried using **carbonized** paper and cardboard for filaments. However, at the time, he couldn't create a good enough vacuum to stop the filaments from burning out. Swan invented a process for making cotton into a special new material that he used for filaments. This was one of the first human-made materials.

Patent problems

Swan and Edison borrowed ideas from each other, and from other inventors. This created problems with patents. In the early 1880s, Edison began making and selling light bulbs in the United Kingdom as well as in the United States. Swan **sued** Edison, saying that Edison's bulbs were the same as the ones in his own patent. Swan won a court battle, and Edison was forced to go into partnership with him. In 1883 they formed the Edison and Swan United Electric Light Company to make and to sell "Ediswan" light bulbs in Britain.

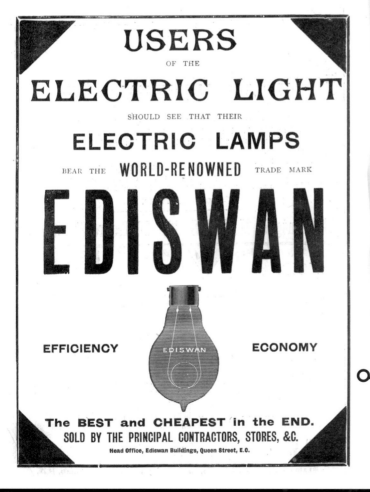

USERS
OF THE
ELECTRIC LIGHT
SHOULD SEE THAT THEIR
ELECTRIC LAMPS
BEAR THE WORLD-RENOWNED TRADE MARK
EDISWAN

EFFICIENCY   EDISWAN   ECONOMY

The BEST and CHEAPEST in the END.
SOLD BY THE PRINCIPAL CONTRACTORS, STORES, &C.
Head Office, Ediswan Buildings, Queen Street, E.C.

Setbacks

Swan was not the only inventor to take Edison to court. Edison fought legal battles with several other people working on their own light bulbs in the United States, United Kingdom, France, and Canada. Sometimes he won, but often he lost.

This is an advertisement for Ediswan light bulbs from 1898.

20

Better bulbs

Modern incandescent light bulbs are almost the same as the bulbs sold by Edison and Swan more than 100 years ago. The only major difference is that modern bulbs use a **tungsten** filament. By 1909 tungsten was used for bulb-making by the General Electric Company in the United States. Tungsten bulbs lasted much longer and were more efficient than carbon bulbs.

The filament of this modern incandescent light bulb is made from tightly coiled tungsten wire.

LIGHT FROM GAS

A gas discharge lamp (also known as a **vapor** lamp) is a glass tube filled with gas. Electricity flowing through the gas makes the gas glow. The color of the light depends on the gas. For example, neon gas gives out red light, and a mixture of argon and **mercury** vapor gives out blue light.

These gas discharge lamps were used to display signs on the front of the London Pavilion movie theater in the 1930s.

In 1902 Frenchman Georges Claude invented a way of getting gases such as neon and argon from the air. Claude investigated these gases and discovered that neon glowed red when electricity flowed through it. He made a neon lamp that became popular for signs. He made his fortune from this idea.

This modern **energy-efficient** bulb is a coiled gas discharge tube.

Inventions

In 1855 a German scientist named Heinrich Geissler demonstrated gas discharge. After this, discharge tubes were known as Geissler tubes. In the 1880s, Geissler tubes were made for entertainment. They made patterns of light that changed when spectators touched them.

The first gas discharge lamp used for lighting was made in 1898. The lamp was made from glass tubes filled with nitrogen or carbon dioxide gas. It was designed by U.S. inventor Daniel McFarlan Moore.

Fluorescent lamps were introduced in the 1930s. A fluorescent lamp has a tube coated inside with a material called phosphor. The gas inside the tube gives out **ultraviolet light**. When the ultraviolet light hits the phosphor, the phosphor glows.

23

1962—Nick Holonyak invents the first **LED** to make red light (see page 24)

1970

LIGHT-EMITTING DIODES

A **light-emitting diode (LED)** is a small electronic device that gives out light. The first LED to give out light (which was red) was invented in 1962 by U.S. scientist Nick Holonyak. These early LEDs were not bright enough for lighting, but they were used as indicator lights on electronic equipment. Holonyak worked at the General Electric Company and is now known as the "father of the LED."

In 1963 he predicted that LEDs would eventually replace **incandescent light bulbs**, and that is beginning to happen today.

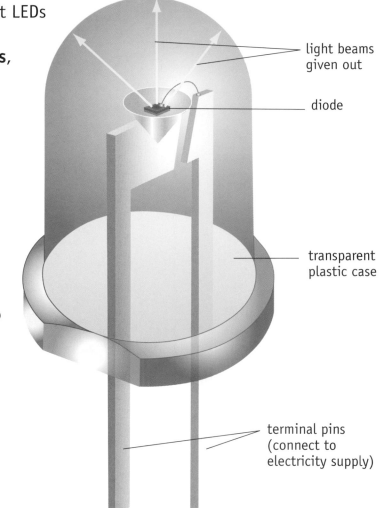

light beams given out

diode

transparent plastic case

terminal pins (connect to electricity supply)

This diagram shows the inside of an LED. The diode gives out light when electricity flows through it.

1980—The Philips company introduces the first successful compact **fluorescent lamp** (see page 27)

EUREKA!

Captain Henry Joseph Round was a British scientist who worked for the radio pioneer Guglielmo Marconi. In 1907 Round was experimenting with radio receivers. He noticed a tiny glow coming from where the end of a thin wire, known as a cat's whisker, was touching a crystal of material. This was the first light-emitting diode, but it was decades before practical LEDs were made.

LED displays showed the results on the first electronic calculator in the 1970s.

LEDs today

Today, we use LEDs in thousands of places: for indicator lights (for, example, on a computer keyboard); for message displays (for example, on buses and trains); for traffic signals; in optical fiber cables; in remote controls; and in displays. Super-bright LEDs are used for lighting in homes and in flashlights.

25

1990

INTO THE FUTURE

Today, people around the world are concerned about a problem called **global warming.** To combat global warming, we must reduce our use of **fossil fuels**. Fossil fuels are burned at electricity generating stations. If we use less electricity, we will not need to burn so much fuel. That is where light bulbs come in.

Compact fluorescent bulbs use less electricity than incandescent bulbs.

Goodbye to incandescent lighting

The **incandescent light bulb** was the main source of light for more than 100 years. But only about 10 percent of the electricity it uses is turned into light. The rest is turned to heat, and is wasted. That is why incandescent bulbs are being replaced by **fluorescent lamps** and **LED** lighting. In some countries, it will soon be against the law to sell incandescent bulbs.

LEDs can be used for decoration as well as lighting, as has been done in this hotel lounge.

Better bulbs

The small fluorescent bulbs that we use in light fittings are called compact fluorescent lamps (CFLs). These were introduced by the Philips company in 1980. CFLs use just 25 percent of the energy of incandescent bulbs, and they last up to 10 times longer.

LED lighting uses the same amount of electricity as fluorescent lighting. LEDs last even longer than fluorescent bulbs—up to an amazing 50,000 hours (that is more than five years). Perhaps in the future a new light bulb will be invented that uses even less electricity.

2009—The European Union bans the sale of 100-watt incandescent light bulbs

2010

TIMELINE

around 70,000 years ago
The first animal fat lamps are used

around 9,000 years ago
Humans invent fire-making tools

around 5,000 years ago
The candle is invented in Egypt

1840s
Joseph Swan makes experimental light bulbs

1830s
Faraday discovers how to make a **dynamo** to produce electricity

1821
Michael Faraday invents the **electric motor**

1855
Heinrich Geissler demonstrates the principle of gas discharge

1860s
The first electricity **generators** are built

1870s
Hermann Sprengel invents his **vacuum** pump

1907
Captain Henry Joseph Round discovers that diodes can give out light

1902
Georges Claude invents a way of getting neon and argon gases from the air

1898
Daniel McFarlan Moore makes the first successful gas discharge lamp

1909
The General Electric Company starts making bulbs with **tungsten** filaments

1910
Claude makes the first neon lamp

1930
Fluorescent lamps are introduced

around 2,000 years ago
Gas is used for lighting in China

1790s
The gas lamp is invented in England

1800
Alesssandro Volta invents the first **battery**

1816
Thomas Drummond invents the limelight

1807
Humphry Davy invents the first electric **arc lamp**

1801
Humphry Davy demonstrates an incandescent lamp

1874
Henry Woodward and Mathew Evans take out a **patent** for a light bulb

1878
Thomas Edison makes a light bulb with a **platinum filament**

1879
Joseph Swan demonstrates his first working light bulb

1883
Thomas Edison and Joseph Swan form the Edison and Swan United Electric Light Company

1882
Edison opens an electricity generating station. Swan starts the Swan Electric Light Company Ltd.

1880
Edison forms the Edison Electric Lamp Company

1962
Nick Holonyak invents the first **LED** to make red light

1980
The Philips company introduces the first successful compact fluorescent lamp

2009
The European Union bans the sale of 100-watt **incandescent light bulbs**

GLOSSARY

arc lamp lamp that makes light from a spark that jumps across a gap between two electrodes

battery device containing different metals immersed in chemicals that gives out electricity

carbonized describes something that has been heated up to turn it into carbon

dynamo device that produces electricity when a coil of wire inside is spun around in a magnetic field

electric motor device that produces movement when it is connected to a supply of electricity

electrode place where electricity is transferred between different points

energy-efficient uses as little energy as possible

filament thin piece of material in an incandescent light bulb that glows when electricity flows through it

fluorescent lamp tube filled with gas and coated inside with phosphor. When electricity passes through the tube, the gas gives out ultraviolet light, which makes the phosphor glow.

fossil fuel fuel made from the remains of ancient plants or animals. Oil, gas, and coal are fossil fuels.

friction force that acts to stop objects that are sliding against each other. Friction can make heat.

fuse safety device that stops electricity from flowing if there is a fault in a machine connected to the electricity supply

generator any device that produces electricity

global warming gradual warming of Earth's atmosphere caused mainly by gases released when we burn fuels

incandescence glow made by something that is very hot

incandescent light bulb lamp that makes light when electricity flows through a thin piece of material inside a glass bulb, making it glow white hot

light-emitting diode (LED) small electronic device that gives out light

lime white, chalky substance made by heating limestone to a very high temperature

mercury silver-colored metal that is normally liquid, often called "quicksilver"

meter device that measures the amount of electricity used by a house or other building

patent license given to an inventor that makes it illegal for somebody else to copy an invention

platinum silver-colored metal

sue take legal action against somebody

tuberculosis disease that infects people's lungs

tungsten hard, gray metal

ultraviolet light sort of light that is invisible to us

vacuum space where there is nothing, not even air

vapor substance in a form similar to a gas

wick piece of string in an oil lamp or candle that soaks up oil or wax. The oil or wax burns at the top of the wick.

30

FIND OUT MORE

Books

Knudsen, Shannon. *Thomas Edison (History Makers)*. Minneapolis: Lerner, 2004.

Matthews, John R. *The Light Bulb (Inventions That Shaped the World)*. New York: Franklin Watts, 2005.

Oxlade, Chris. *Inventors' Secret Scrapbook (Crabtree Connections)*. New York: Crabtree, 2011.

Websites

www.ge.com/company/history/edison.html
Find out about Thomas Edison and how he founded the General Electric company.

www.thomasedison.org
For lots more information about Edison, go to the Thomas Edison Innovation Foundation website.

Places to visit

The Thomas Edison Center at Menlo Park
37 Christie Street
Edison, New Jersey 08820
www.menloparkmuseum.org
This museum explores the burst of creativity Thomas Edison experienced beginning in 1876, when he set up facilities in Menlo Park, New Jersey.

Edison and Ford Winter Estates Museum
2350 McGregor Boulevard
Fort Myers, Florida 33901
www.efwefla.org
Visit Thomas Edison's home in Florida and one of his laboratories. There is also a museum with many exhibits exploring Edison's inventions, including many examples of his development of the light bulb.

INDEX